Bring a Dead Mouse
The Secret to Finding Your Perfect Job

Revised and Expanded

by Charlotte A. Lee

B.A.D. Mouse Publishing, Inc.
2014

For my amazing clients-thank you
for your trust and friendship

ISBN Print: 978-0-9905353-0-0
ISBN ebook: 978-0-9905353-1-7

Printed in the United States of America

First Edition, February 2011
Second Edition, July 2014

Design and Layout: Rick Soldin (book-comp.com)

www.BringADeadMouse.com

Contents

Notes

A Brief—but Important Note: What's the Deal with Dead Mice?

The phrases "bring a dead mouse" and "finding a job" aren't typically found in the same paragraph, and I'm pretty sure they've never been seen side by side in the title of a book. But hang in there with me for a minute and I'll explain.

My mom used to tell me that when she was growing up in Charlotte, North Carolina, the family's pet cats would occasionally drop dead mice at her feet when she stepped out of her door to go to school. At first, she was disgusted (who wouldn't be?). But she eventually realized that those mice were actually presents, the cats' special way of showing her they were thinking of her. Yuck.

v

But my mom (or was it the cats?) had a point. One of the most powerful techniques you can use in your job search is to make yourself memorable. And one of the most powerful ways of making yourself memorable is to bring small "gifts" to the people you're meeting with. Later on in this book, we'll talk more about how to select the best dead mouse. But let me leave you with a phrase that every client I've ever worked with has heard me say at least once: "Memorable is hire-able." And that's what this book is all about.

In addition, sometimes you're in a role and just not happy or don't think it is using all your skills or going anywhere. This book and some of the tips and techniques can help you manage your professional growth, explore a new industry or help you get engaged again. According to Gallup's 2013 State of the American Workplace report, 70% of U.S. employees are either "not engaged" or "actively disengaged" at work. And the Harris Interactive Survey showed 55% of working adults are in search of a new profession. If this is you, read on!

Preface

Every once in a while a singular event changes our lives. As a nation, we might think back to Hurricane Katrina, the Financial Crisis, or the attack on the World Trade Towers. As individuals we are galvanized—that is, shocked into taking action—by the loss of a loved one, the loss of a home, or the loss of a job. In such cases we search for something that inspires us to rediscover our courage and move forward. It might be the memory of a fireman raising the flag over the smoldering rubble of a once proud building. It might be encouragement from a friend or colleague. Or it might come from reading a powerful book that fits the needs of the moment. A book that allows you to view the galvanizing event from a different perspective. A book that causes you to stop and reconsider your situation and your options. A book that gives you hope. A book that you will one day reopen and find yourself thinking, this was the turning point that led to my eventual success.

Charlotte Lee's book offers readers just such a turning point. She is, in fact, one of those rare human beings who not only knows her subject matter inside and out, but is able to put straightforward, actionable advice on the page. Her wisdom will be of particular interest to those who insist on looking for jobs for which they are uniquely qualified—or put another way, jobs that will allow them to use their talents to resolve important problems for their prospective employers. Attempting to serve that small, vital part of the workforce, Ms. Lee teaches us that a job search is as much about your prospective employer's needs as it is about your own qualifications.

Read it and profit.

David X Martin
Published risk expert and author

Introduction

Why This Book?

Every morning, on my way to work, I walk past the New York Public Library, the building flanked by two enormous lions, Patience and Fortitude. And every morning I'm reminded that searching for a job—particularly in this economy—takes exactly those two qualities: patience and fortitude.

According to ExecuNet, a job-search website for senior executives, if you're trying to find an executive-level job, you can expect to spend a little over 10 months looking. And the U.S. Department of Labor says that the average unemployed person spends 27 weeks looking for a job. Based on my experience working with thousands of executives, that number is dead on. You'll need a lot of patience and fortitude to keep focused on your search for that amount of time. And you'll need even more to cope with the warped sense of time that job hunting creates.

There are two time zones: one for those who are working and one for those out of work. It goes like this: You send an email to a hiring manager and expect a timely response. But your definition of timely and the manager's probably aren't the same. For you, 24 hours seems about right. Maybe 48. Any more than that will seem like foreeeeever. But for the manager, a week might be rushing it. So take a deep breath and try to relax. It can sometimes take as many as seven attempts before you actually make contact with the person you're trying to reach. A job search is a marathon, not a sprint.

Remember when you were working full-time? You may not have been as responsive to every call and email as you should have, so try to be patient. Sometimes it's is really not about you. I remember speaking with a client and he mentioned how he had never responded to recruiters' or headhunters' calls. But now, he was annoyed at their unresponsiveness towards him! What goes around, comes around, I am afraid.

Being unemployed or underemployed—especially if it lasts the better part of a year—can be extremely demoralizing. The Great Recession that began in 2008 (and continues to this day) has created perhaps the most difficult job market in over 20 years. To start with, our economy is on somewhat shaky ground. Plus, there are fewer large companies and more niche players. There are 15 million Americans out of work and nearly nine million fewer jobs out there than just a few years ago. And the competition for those jobs is fiercer than ever. The good old days when all you had to do to get a job was match up the skills on your resume to an online job spec are long gone. And they're not coming back any time soon. In addition, when I surveyed my last 81 clients, only one is working for an old boss from 20 years ago. That means your new boss/hiring manager will probably be a stranger to you. That's why you have to get outside your network and meet with your network's network and venture out further afield than ever.

Today, Human Resources experts say they hire fewer than five percent of applicants. And why not? Hiring is now a buyer's market. The applicant pool is well stocked with highly qualified people with powerful skills and impressive CVs. Not surprisingly, employers have raised their expectations for applicants. Hiring managers tend to be conservative, holding out for candidates clearly able to do the job—usually candidates who've already done the job successfully elsewhere else. In the new paradigm, you need to establish your value in the marketplace. To do that, you need to listen actively to potential employers about what's keeping them up at night. Then you need to figure out which of your skills will fix their problem and how you're going to persuade them to hire you as either a contractor or full time. You've got to show them you can help them meet the challenges they face.

The path between you and your next job is a numbers game, pure and simple: She/he with the most face-to-face meetings wins. Why? First, because face-to-face interviews give you valuable practice, and by the time you get to the hiring manager, you're a rock star. Second, because the more people you speak with, the better the chance that you'll hit on one who has a problem you can help solve. You can shape your job search and its outcome by how you choose to approach it, focusing on the approach that will most increase your likelihood of success. The more people you know within an organization, the better your campaign to work there will be. The trick is to get those people to start creating some buzz about you.

There are two sure-fire ways to sink your search. First, be alone, second, be on-line more than two hours per day. Instead, go out and meet some people, because *people* hire people. No one's going to hire you based on an online resume or a phone call. You'll get hired only after someone meets you face to face and discovers that you have both the skills and the personality to be successful in their firm. Not convinced by how important face-to-face meetings are? Consider this: According to the 2013 Job Outlook Survey by the National Association of Colleges and Employers, the number one skill employers want from their new hires is the "ability to verbally communicate with persons inside and outside the organization."

The biggest predictor of job-hunting success? Optimism. Staying positive, keeping your chin up, and your energy and expectations high will take all the fortitude you can muster. Finding that optimism within yourself will allow you to go out into the world, connect with the right people and find the job you want and deserve.

So how do I know all this, and what qualifies me to write a book on job hunting? Well, I'm a Senior Vice President with Lee Hecht Harrison, the largest outplacement firm in the world, with over 350 offices in 85 countries. In this role, I coach senior executives in a variety of industries, including legal, financial, consumer, telecom, media, pharma, and professional services. Perhaps more important than any of that, I'm a career coach with a winning record. Ninety-eight percent of my clients have found jobs. Ninety-eight percent. In fact, I've been doing this for so long—and so successfully—that many of my old clients are hiring my new ones!

There's no shortage of job search books, websites, and other resources out there. And there's no question that some of them can be quite helpful. However, times have changed since even the best of them were written. Today, experts say that we'll have at least ten jobs in our working life. Six of them will not be of our choosing. They'll be jobs we find because the last one came to an end for one reason or another.

The job-hunting landscape—the buyer's market paradigm—isn't going to change anytime soon. I believe that what people really need these days are solid, practical job-search ideas and approaches. In other words, a real "how-to" rather than a "what" or "why" kind of book. And that's exactly what you're going to get in these pages. You'll hear from real, formerly out-of-work professionals how they found new roles and successfully transitioned back to work. And you'll get the specific tools and strategies you can use to land *your* next job—regardless of where you're located or what industry you're targeting.

The book is divided into ten chapters, each one designed to get you closer to your ultimate goal. Each chapter delivers a clear message. But all told, this small book is greater than the sum of its chapters. I know it's tempting to skip around, but try to go through the chapters in order. You'll be a lot happier with the results.

A couple of last minute thoughts which you will read more about in the coming pages. Every day, you have to be the solution to a business problem faced by a prospective employer. Make sure your generosity shines through. Sometimes it's just a kind word, quick email or phone call, a card dropped in the mail randomly or a text that took you three seconds to send. Whatever it is, do it. You're creating positive karma around yourself and people will remember you well. If you do one a day, that's 365 positive items out there in the Universe about you. Wow!

Now, let's get started!

Notes

Chapter 1

Know—and Differentiate—Thyself

If you're ever going to have even the slimmest chance of standing out in a crowded marketplace, it's essential that you have a solid understanding of who you are, what you do well, and how to brand and differentiate yourself.

On the most basic level, differentiation is your ability to be memorable. And memorable is hire-able. Think about it this way: After you've had your interviews and walked out of the room, what will people remember? They'll remember that the procurement guy was a former Navy officer, that the banker with the blond hair is fluent in Mandarin, that Roger was a Rhodes Scholar, Aisha is a designer (but a lawyer by training), Rob is an Eagle Scout, Karen is an MBA, CFA, and CPA, and Peter is a Master Black Belt in Six Sigma. These are all great differentiators—making these candidates unique and stand out from the crowd. And that's a good thing, given that this is a buyer's market, where employers can frankly get exactly whom and what they want in an employee.

So what will people remember about you?

The things that make you memorable—the things that make you uniquely "you," are your brand, and you want to make sure you've got two of them: a professional one and a personal one. They should be different from each other, but should each reflect a skill or something unique about you that the company you're interviewing needs.

One important thing to remember about brands—personal as well as professional—is that they *respond* to a need—they rarely ever *create* a need. Think Mercedes versus Porsche; Harvard versus Princeton; Goldman Sachs versus Bank of America. Each one of those brands—and that's exactly what they are—is built around responding to the needs of a particular segment of the larger market-place. Let me give you another example. Toyota has a very strong brand, but they recognized that most people look-ing to buy a luxury car would drive right past the Toyota dealership. So they created Lexus, a purely luxury brand. Similarly, hip, young car buyers would have driven right past the Toyota dealership—after all, Toyota was their *par-ents'* car company. So Toyota created Scion.

Toyota clearly understands its brands—including their potential and their limitations—extremely well. And before you can find your next job, you're going to have to develop a thorough grasp of your own personal brand. What specific need is your brand responding to and how are you uniquely qualified to satisfy it? (In marketing terms, what's your value proposition or unique selling proposition?) This isn't a step you can take lightly or skip over. In my view, it's the foundation for everything you'll ever do in your career, and the most difficult part of the job-search process. It's how you articulate who you are, and how you can present the value-added you bring to any potential employer.

Your personal brand is made up of three distinct components, which, together, I call your *inventory*.

◊ Your skill sets

◊ Your operating style

◊ Your personal style

Let's take a look at each one in a bit more detail.

Identifying your skill sets is pretty easy. Are you a CPA, FP&A, COO, CEO, CFA, operations expert, IT guru, project manager, etc.? My lovely client Elaine has 11 certifications. She's a knowledge expert with very impressive credentials in the increasingly important, and highly technical, field of information management. Those certifications get that message across. But whether you have initials after your name or you've earned some kind of official certification, the process is the same: Come up with a detailed list of everything you actually do—*all* of your skills. Do you manage people, analyze data, reduce costs, streamline processes, generate revenues, develop strategies, or market products? Great, write it down. And don't limit yourself to my list. This process is about you, so think about all of your skills—even the ones that you may not think are business-related. One of Jeff's best skills was mentoring junior professionals at the firm. And Michael is especially adept at explaining complex financial structures in a way that even non-finance people can easily understand them. Know your strengths and weaknesses and be able to articulate them clearly and simply with impact.

Your operating style is a description of the way you work. Ask yourself these questions (and get a good handle on the answers, since you'll probably get asked many of the same questions in job interviews!): are you collaborative or dictatorial? Do you work better alone or on a team? How do others perceive you—whether they're junior or senior to you? What would your last boss say about you? How would they describe the way you work? What do you think you're known for? Are you the go-to person or an impediment to the process? Part of the solution or part of the problem? In this job market (and any other time, for that matter) you must come to the table with *solutions*. You need to be a problem solver.

If you've never been assessed or gone through a 360 evaluation, consider completing a Myers Briggs-type assessment which you can find free online. Also ask others for feedback and be open to it. Just take it in; don't say anything, get defensive, or get upset or they'll stop speaking. Remember, your eyes and body language give away your emotions. So control your fidgeting, smile, and lean forward—no arms crossed and no furrowed brow. Most of us aren't as self-aware as we think we are. One day I was speaking with my deputy, Ro, and said, "Isn't it great that my office door is open and that I'm using Jack Welch's Management by Walking Around style and casually chatting with folks"? Ro laughed and said, "When people see your door open and hear you coming out, they run! They're petrified of you!" I was stunned. It was clearly time to slow down, smile more, ask more questions, and soften my approach! That's something I work on *every single day*!

Your personal style is a deceptively simple component of your brand, but you'll have a terrible time finding a job if you can't identify it. Are you formal or informal? Conservative or liberal? Extroverted or introverted? The life of the party or a wallflower? Picture a bright light and a bunch of moths moving towards it. Are you the light or the moth? Do people move towards you or are you the one who moves?

In the old Human Resources adage, "can do, will do, fit," this is the fit part. We're in a buyers' market, and *everyone* out there has the skills ("can do") and desire ("will do") to do the job. But what companies are looking for is someone who'll mesh seamlessly with their existing structure. Someone who will successfully leverage the company's brand/product and grow their business. This is a "fit" market. No one has the time or the patience to deal with prima donnas, high-maintenance employees, or difficult personalities. The Great Recession and the painfully slow recovery in its wake, has provided the perfect cover for employers looking to get rid of employees who just don't fit.

The current market calls for a lot of flexibility on the job seeker's part. Of course, you want to be authentic, but you also have to build an excellent rapport with everyone you interview with. These days, when most hiring is done by consensus, you may need to get more than a dozen people to like you and want you on board. Modify your behavior to fit with the person you're meeting with. It's not enough to know what you did, do, or want. You need to evaluate your audience, learn what they need, and move to it. That includes the receptionist and the assistant. One of my clients, Mike, once started a network conversation with someone, and ended up with a job. When they told him what their challenge was, Mike responded with a solution he had implemented in a previous role—and it worked!

Have the same level of respect for each person. You do not want to be seen as elitist, so treat everyone the same. You never know how any one person's opinion will impact the decision to hire you—or not.

Overall, your brand should reflect a distinctive combination of skill sets or something unique about you that the company you're interviewing needs. Unfortunately, it's hard to predict what that's going to be. Most people who meet me remember I was President of Habitat for Humanity in Nassau County, not the investment banking firms I worked for. Go figure. You just don't know what will stand out. But as long as you *do* stand out, it's okay. Remember to trot out a few things in case the one you love is not the one that resonates with your audience.

Once you've spent some time considering the three facets of your inventory and putting everything down on paper, it's time to start mapping out your plan of attack.

Chapter 2

Embracing Risk:
Courage as a Skill Set

Finding a job is one of the hardest things you'll ever do. Harder than getting married, harder than having a baby, and even harder than raising a child. Why is job hunting so difficult? In my view, the two biggest reasons are (1) you'll need to take risks—something most people dread, and (2) it requires asking for help—something very few people feel comfortable doing. Fortunately, both of these skills are easily learned.

Let's start with taking risks. Actually, let's talk about complacency, which is the *opposite* of taking risks. Complacency often feels pretty comfortable and may even make you feel secure in your current situation. So what does complacency look like? Well, it's when you keep on doing things the way you've always done them, and you never do anything to make yourself memorable or invaluable. So if you arrive and leave at the same time every day, wear the same type of outfits, eat lunch at the same time and with the same people, and you don't volunteer for new projects, organize the Holiday party, get to know the new hires, or go out of your way to impress your boss, you're being complacent. And the big problem with complacency is that it never lasts. If you're complacent in your job, you won't be there for long. If you're complacent in your job search, you're going to be out of work a lot longer than necessary.

Think about it this way: When you're employed, you're taking frequent, small risks over a long period of time. When you are out of work, you need to take larger risks over a shorter period of time.

Taking risks in your job search means getting out of your comfort zone and doing things a little (or a lot) differently. When was the last time you had a great idea—and actually shared it with other people? Have you ever spoken up in a job forum to ask a question? Have you taken the initiative and offered to mentor a junior person, or asked a senior person out to lunch? Have you organized a community service day or event for your firm? Have you introduced yourself to the new guy—and everyone else on your floor?

The key to getting out of your comfort zone is to take small steps. With each step, that zone gets a little bigger and a little wider, and the more you do, the more you'll find you *can* do. Take a small step today! You'll be moving in a wider zone tomorrow.

Every time you speak to a stranger, call up a colleague you haven't seen in years, or send an invite to someone on LinkedIn you barely know, you're taking a risk.

There's no question that rejection can sting. But, really and truly, what's the worst they can do? Ignore you or say "No." So what? As my mother-in-law often said, "It's not a train wreck!" No harm, no foul, so just move on. At least 80 percent of the time, it's not personal—they don't hate you. It's just that they don't have (or can't make) the time right now; everyone's being asked to do more with less. Suffering this kind of rejection—and learning that the world hasn't come to an end—will actually strengthen you and give you the courage you'll need to take *more*—and bigger—risks in the future. So rather than take the rejection personally, just move on.

Now that you've got a handle on risk taking, let's move on to something that may scare more people than the possibility of rejection: asking for help. Asking for help can be a scary thing to contemplate, let alone do. The most effective way to reduce the scariness of asking for help is to consciously start helping *other* people as much as you can. It's a little like being The Godfather. You do favors and perform services for people all the time. It could be as small as making an introduction for them or being a reference or carpooling one day per week. Then, one day, when *you* need something, you can ask for it without feeling like a leech or a loser. In a sense, you're not actually *asking* for anything—it's almost as if you're collecting on a debt. (And the truth is that most people really do want to help you.) So, from now on, make the business of helping others a priority in your life. Our society is built on reciprocity. We've all heard the old adage, one hand washes the other. You go first, and others will reciprocate. And remember: when you land in your new job, pay it forward. What goes around, really does come around.

If you happen to be out of work, take a quick look at Chapter 6, on dead mice, and start coming up with some dead mice of your own. This is a world of reciprocity and if you don't give, you won't get. Sometimes people just need a how're-you-doing email, or a little help with a net-working issue, or an idea at work, or an article on something that fits their world. You want to have been leaving lots of dead mice on everyone's doorsteps all year round, so when it is your turn to ask for something, it won't seem strained. If you're trying to get a meeting with a specific person, track down some information you know he or she would find particularly interesting. It could be an article about something he personally or professionally cares about. Or some news about a person she knows. Maybe her child needs help with college essays and you're a terrific writer. Or maybe his wife is sick and you can deliver chicken soup to the house. Or a spouse is out of work and you can help him line up some networking meetings at your former company. You get the point.

Looking for a job is an activity that takes a ton of resilience and patience. You'll hear, "No, I can't see you," "No, I don't know anyone you can speak with," and "No, you didn't get the job." Over and over and over, for months at a time. After every one of these knock-downs, you're going to have to pick yourself up, brush yourself off, and start all over again. You'll end up kissing a lot of frogs to get that prince or princess. But all it takes is one. My client Sara had 167 meetings, but only one got her the job. But since neither you nor I know which one it will be, we have to do a great job with every one of them. Please do consider re-scheduling a meeting if you don't think you're able to bring your A game.

You have the talent, the knowledge, and the experience. All you need to do now, is hang in there until you accomplish your goal it's only one job—you can do this!

My client, Peter, had been a C-Suite executive for many years before losing his job. One afternoon, Peter came to my office and joined a group of 20 other out-of-work clients. Frustrated and angry, he slammed his hand on the conference table and said, "Dammit, I'm a senior guy and I expect people to call me back." Then, with eyes boring into the faces of all the startled candidates, he rather sheepishly added, "Boy, did I have to get over that pretty quickly." It would be great if everyone returned your calls and offered to do things for you (in the same way that you're selflessly doing things for others). But don't hold your breath. Sad, but true.

Many people find that their immediate network is actually a lot less helpful than they had expected, and that instead, it's the random acts of kindness from strangers that make the difference. Or a friend of a friend or a friend. Always ask the person you're meeting with or speaking with, whether there's anyone else they would be able to connect you with. Name a company or two to make it easier for people to help you. Or name a specific function ("Do you know any lawyers/real estate people/people in not-for-profits?") It's time to leave that ego at the door and start asking for—and accepting—help. After all, you know that if someone asked you for help, you'd honestly try. There *are* people out there who are in a position to do something for you, but in most cases, they won't offer unless you come right out and ask. Sometimes, that's simply because they don't know you need any help, or they don't know exactly how to help. You're going to have to come up with creative ways to ask, follow up, ask again, and thank them. Most importantly, when you *do* get that great job (and I know you will), please remember to pay it forward—in other words, do something for someone else *before* they ask you.

For those people in jobs where they are not happy, consider taking the time to link in to long lost friends, bosses, and colleagues—not just people you know from your most recent job. Spruce up your Linkedin profile with an updated photo and your latest news. Send out a "Have a great week; would love to reconnect" linkedin message with your contact info and see if anyone comes back to you—voila! Some catch-up meetings will now transpire. Call a friend (not email …) who works for a company you admire. Ask good questions; see him/her for coffee. Email four or five people this month to "check in" and see how they are doing. Start making these outreaches now when you don't need anything and can just listen to them vent etc. On your existing role, think of ways you can improve your situation. Is it more communication with your peers, boss or other departments? Should you be asking to be on more assignments, different, more interesting projects, so you are sharpening or expanding your skills? Is there a conference you would like to attend and represent the firm? Is there one where you should be a speaker or panelist? Can you or should you volunteer just so you can be seen and see others? It's on YOU to start making your job better by opening and improving your communications. Remember, you cannot change others, only you. Walk over to someone today and start improving your day-to-day job.

Twenty seconds of courage. That's all you need to send that email, make that call, have that ask, meet that person, go through that door. It is never going to be completely easy but the more you do it, the better and more empowered you'll feel and the more progress you'll make in the search and in life—life takes risks. This is a 20 second risk. Twenty seconds. Come on! You can do it!

Notes

Chapter 3

Tools of the Trade

Most job seekers spend a lot of time writing, formatting, and polishing their resume. But, while there's no question that resumes are important, they're just one of the many tools you'll need if you're going to get the job you want with the employer you want to work with. Essential tools of the job search trade include your resume, your "elevator pitch" or positioning statement, email address (your name), salary requirements, note cards (for old fashioned thank you notes), business cards, bullet points to highlight your strengths, and references. Additional tools are increasingly important as well. These include your Linkedin profile, (Facebook too depending upon your sector), a one paragraph profile, a professional-quality headshot, a single, phone number where you're reachable 24/7, a personalized URL, and an Advisory Board to keep you on track. Let's take a look at each of these tools in a little more detail.

Resume (or CV)

Two pages max, written with a 10-point Times New Roman or another easy-to-read font. Anything smaller than that is too hard to read—especially by people who pore over dozens of resumes every day. Hard-to-read resumes usually turn into unread resumes. Also, make sure your resume is in pdf format so that whenever you email it to anyone you'll know it'll look perfect when they open it.

Resume must-haves include: your full name, mailing address, email address, LinkedIn address, and cell phone number. In the Experience section, go back only 15 years. If you've been in the labor force longer than that, put in a section called Other Work Experience and just list the firm, your job title, and a one-line description. You don't need to list the specific years you were at each position in this section.

One resume must-have that most people overlook is ease of navigation. You're trying to draw people to the page, and an overly dense document with no white space is a turn-off. Remember, a resumé is a marketing document, not a list of everything you've done for the past 25 years. Your ability to differentiate yourself in this crowded marketplace depends on your ability to clearly and concisely talk about you accomplishments.

Towards the end of the resume (bottom of page 2), be sure to include an Additional Information section, which is for things about you that don't specifically fit anywhere else but make you an interesting candidate. For example, you've lived and worked in the US, Asia, and Europe; you speak French and Spanish; you founded an investment club for inner-city kids, and so on. The Additional Information section is also where you articulate how well you "fit" with the organization you're applying to (see Chapter 1 for more on this). Companies (and the individuals who work there) tend to hire people they like, who look a bit like them, who share similar values and interests. This section, while it may not seem terribly important, is actually a very valuable screening tool as well as a place to add some interesting "mutual interest" possibilities. For example, if the hiring manager you're meeting with is big on mentoring, and you've been active with Big Brothers, Big Sisters, you've just differentiated yourself from a whole bunch of other people. If the head of HR believes in public school education and you volunteer for Learning Leaders in the schools and became a Certified Literacy Tutor, you've just leapt ahead of your competition. So if you aren't already doing so, start thinking about causes that you believe in, and start giving back. It's great for the people you're helping, but helping others will make you feel great too. All it takes is a few hours a month. Give to get.

Elevator pitch and verbal positioning

One of the most important parts of any job search is getting the word out. Do not hide. Tell everyone you know that you're looking for your next great opportunity! That will force you to get your pitch down—nothing slows the wheels of progress more quickly than telling someone that you'll get back to them. You need to tell them right now. The elevator pitch is a quick, concise statement of who you are, what you've done, and what you want to do next. "I'm Sue Smith, a financial planning and analysis expert, most recently out of ABC company. They went through a major restructuring and eliminated my position, but it was a great place to work and I got some valuable experience there. Fortunately, my skills are fully transferable and I have excellent references, too." Your verbal positioning answers the question, "So why did you leave your last employer?" before they ask it. Usurping this question is a better approach.

Be sure to customize your elevator pitch for your audience and give specifics when appropriate. For example, if Sue is meeting with a CFO, she could say "I've worked with 3 CFO's in my previous roles, and some of the items I prepared for them, were … . Might those be helpful to you?" With a bit of luck, this will pique her interest and she'll begin to brainstorm a bit with Sue—or at least give her some additional color on the role and the challenges the firm faces.

My client, John, has been using his elevator pitch to introduce himself to people during department meetings and one-on-one meetings with senior managers. Having practiced and refined it has made him able to present himself naturally and credibly to anyone anywhere. I often put clients in groups so we can practice (with strangers, as they do not know each other at first) and get constructive feedback on how they look and sound. Nothing warms my heart more than to hear a client tell another how much she/he has progressed from the first time they heard the pitch. Barbara told Laura, "Wow! You sound great now … Sooooo much better than last time!" Laura beamed, by the way. We all like an attaboy sometimes. Stu and John rarely smiled. Now that that's been brought to their attention, we discovered that they both had teeth and gums galore! Oh—and the room lights up when they smile.

Email address

What we're doing here is reinforcing your branding, so try to include your actual name (joansmith@gmail.com). I recommend that you use Gmail (or, if you're fewer than five years out of school, your alumni.edu address is fine too). AOL screams "dated," and Hotmail and Yahoo! are close behind. Make sure the same email address appears on your resume, note cards, cover letters, and business cards if you have more than one email account (and who doesn't these days?) be sure you set them up so they all forward to a single address.

Cover letter

Short and sweet letters work best. In the first paragraph, clearly say why you're writing, and be sure to include the title or type of job you're applying for. In the second paragraph, briefly talk about a few of the ways your skills and experience align perfectly with the job. Use some of the language in the job spec in your letter. Be sure to personalize it if at all possible. Think about ways you can be an extra pair of hands. What's keeping them up at night? How can you help? In the third paragraph, you'll thank the person you're writing to for his or her time and consideration. If you're emailing your cover letter, make sure the letter itself is in the body of the email, *not* an attachment, and that you include only one link—the one that opens your resume. One click is all you get.

Salary requirements

A lot of employers request this information because it allows them to screen out people who are asking for way too much, are too senior or who don't know what they're worth. If at all possible, try to get a salary range from the employer. You may be able to find that information on the company's website, job listings, a compensation website like glassdoor.com or from someone you know who works there. If you can't find out the actual range, you'll have to come up with one of your own. A place to start is with the salary (not including any bonuses) that you earned at your previous job. If your earnings were all over the place, list an average for the past three years. In person or on the phone you can always turn a "what kind of salary are you expecting?" or "how much did you make last year," question into "what's the range?" But unless you absolutely have to, *do not* include specific salary requirements in cover letters, on applications, or in any other written communication unless you absolutely have to.

Note cards

You'll use note cards when you send handwritten thank-you's to your centers of influence (people who have really gone above and beyond for you, or who might do so), as well as to accompany items you're sending to remind folks of who you are (all of this, of course, is in addition to the Thanksgiving or Holiday cards you usually send out). For example, a manager you met with spent some time talking about her recent trip to Versailles, and you follow up with an article you came across on the same topic. Sending something of interest to people you have met recently is a wonderful way to keep your name fresh in their memory and remind them that you're still out there—without actually saying anything about yourself or asking for anything. This is a subtle, yet very powerful technique. Be sure the cards you buy are classic and lovely but not over the top. My client Elizabeth thought that the red print of her name, plus the red border on the card and the red lining of the envelope was too much, and just took the lining out. The cards were perfect then! Remember, less is more. Someone sent me a Christmas card and inside the envelope was her husband's business card—he sells real estate ... I don't recommend mixed messages.

Business cards

Although people think of business cards as one of the first things you get after you *start* a job, I think they're also one of the first things to get when you *lose* your job. It's so much easier to ask for someone's business card if you're in the process of handing them yours. You don't want to start a conversation with, "I'm out of work," but you do want, by the end of the conversation, to know what the other person does and for him or her to know what you do and that you're looking for a new role. *Everyone* should have a business card, whether you just got out of college, are hoping to retire soon, or anything in between, have a card and collect as many as you can from others.

Your cards should be printed on white or off-white, good quality card stock. Yes, you may be able to take advantage of some of the "free" business cards some online printers offer, but stay far, far away if the price of "free" is putting an advertising message for the printer on the back of the card. In comes across as really cheap and unprofessional (plus, some people may use the back of your business card to jot down things they want to remember about you: where you met, what line of work you're in, and so on). Ditto for any wild colors or scents. If you're a designer or a marketing professional, you can do something unique as a way of making your business cards stand out from the pile. A little color is okay—maybe a light blue line under your name, a red square above your name, or navy blue ink instead of black. Some color; nothing crazy. The more creative your field, the more color you can get away with. My client, Victoria's, card had her name in fuchsia with a fuchsia back. It looked great and stood out in a good way. But this is about differentiating yourself, *not* making a political statement. Use the same color scheme, font, and logo if you use one (tasteful, original, not a piece of cute clip art you found on the Net) on all your printed materials.

Print the cards with the name people call you: Sandy Smith, not J.T. Sanford Lee Smith-Bell, VII. The address where you live and where you'll be commuting from is important. If nothing else, it's a mutual-interest point ("Oh, you live in Alexandria? So does my brother"). Since you're looking for work at this point and don't have an actual job title, list something like, "Human Resources Executive" or "Finance Professional" under your name. And always include professional credentials, such as CPA, SPHR, or ESQ, but skip educational ones (BA, BS or MBA). Make sure your LinkedIn address ends with your name and not a bunch of numbers. Keep the design of the card very basic, something like this (although you don't have to put your full address on your business card if you're uncomfortable with that):

Charlize Weber, Esq.

101 Road Circle
Anytown, Anywhere 03322
(917) 555-5555

charlizeweber@gmail.com
www.linkedin.charlizeweber.com

Companies I have used in the past include Vistaprint, PrintPlace, Moo, and Morning Print.

Bullets

Use these in lieu of resumes. Craft a set of bullet points to convey your brand—to highlight key aspects of who you are. When you're reaching out to introduce yourself to someone, remember to keep it short. One of the biggest mistakes you can make at this stage of your job search is to use your resume as your calling card—especially for informational meetings. Once people see a resume, they immediately switch to "Oh-no-this-is-about-a-job" mode, and they're likely to brush you off with something designed to get you out of their office: "Sorry, we don't have a job like that," or "I'll send it around" (which is code for "I'll send it to HR where they'll probably lose it under a pile of other unsolicited resumes," or "I'll give it to Bob in accounting and you'll be *his* problem from now on"). That doesn't do much for you, but it makes the person who did it feel a little better about herself because she did *something* for you … Give your target people something about you so they can easily "pitch" you to someone else and introduce you without much trouble. Our job is to make it simple and easy for people to help us and introduce us to others.

When you're doing informational interviews, you're there to gather information, receive advice and guidance, learn about their business, and get to know a company's people and culture. So instead of pulling out your resume, you should put together three bullet points instead. These are short statements that describe you (for example: "12 years as an ABC exec," "CFO and Finance Director," "Colby College undergrad and Wharton MBA," "Operations manager with expertise in clearing and client account management").

My client Rich chose to ignore this piece of advice, and insisted on leading with his resume. He talked about his background and his job search on every phone call and followed up with a resume. He was out of work—and barely had any meetings with anyone—for nine long months, before he finally switched to bullets and almost immediately started landing face-to-face meetings. You absolutely *must* get this right. Looking for a job is one of the hardest things you'll ever do. Trust me. I've done it more than a few times myself and I've coached thousands of clients through the process. Write your bullets out and have them at the ready in case someone says "Send your resume over."

If you hear that, you want to respond with something like this: "May I send some quick bullets instead? I know there are very few roles, and who has time to read a resume? If at all possible, I'd just love to get a short face-to-face meeting to introduce myself, get a little advice and perspective, and widen my network."

Examples of these bullets might be:

◊ Ex-ABC company for 8 years

◊ Ex-DEF company for 6 years

◊ Project manager and product specialist

◊ Bachelor of Science in Engineering, AAA University

◊ PMI Certified; Six Sigma Green Belt

Use your bullets to make it easy for people to introduce you to their network. Do *not* hand out your resume as your calling card. Less is more. Just send your bullets to folks and ask for a 15-minute meeting to network and get advice. Do *not* mention a job—right now all we're doing is trying to open doors, widen our network, practice our elevator pitch, and build rapport. The easier you make it for people, the more likely they'll want to help you. People are consistently being asked to do more with less. Help them help you. Here's an example of the kind of email you'll want to send.

Here's a sample email:

Subject: My friend Charlotte

Hi Steve,
Hope you're well and that the Jets have a better season next year! I was wondering if you would be willing to have a short networking meeting with my friend Charlotte? She was most recently with ABC company (more info below) and just wanted to get some advice about CDE company and you.

Thanks and best,
Laura
(444) 444-4444

References

Be sure you have three to six references from previous roles. Ideally, you'll have a diverse group so that each one can cover different territory. This will let prospective employers know you can work with all kinds of people in all kinds of situations. Contact your references ahead of time to go over the points you want them to cover. After you speak with them on the phone, do send a follow up email thanking them for being your reference and reiterating what the two of you spoke about and what their sound bites are. Try not to use the same people over and over again. When providing reference lists to prospective employers, be sure to include only their personal email addresses and cell phones rather than their work ones where there are restrictions on what they may or may not say during their business day, utilizing their firm's resources. Do include context for the readers so they know if the reference is a colleague, peer, manager, boss, or someone else.

More Essential Tools for Everyday Presentation

A LinkedIn profile. More and more headhunters are dispensing with their own databases and using LinkedIn instead. Your LinkedIn profile should be at least 90 percent complete, include a photo, and mention 6–8 business-related groups that you're a member of, and leave your more recent employer as "current" for 90 days after you've left. You'll also want to Include several recommendations (proof them yourself first *before* the person uploads it to your profile page). And, if anyone ever offers to write a recommendation for you, say Yes. One last word on recommendations. I've been known, when in doubt, to ask recommenders to use only their first name and last initial. That way, if that person is a polarizing figure in your marketplace, there won't be any negative spillover on you. My client Brandon said he could have an extremely senior person at a large investment banking firm, give him a recommendation. Unfortunately, there are a lot of people who aren't crazy about that particular senior executive.

Melina is an over-50 client who didn't have a LinkedIn profile when she started her search. But by the time she left our practice and landed a job, she had more than 200 connections and a great photo up. Do *not* underestimate the importance of this online tool! If you're not already there, get on, get a pic up, and get started making connections! Five hundred connections is a good number to shoot for.

Bio. This is something you'll need to come up with anyway, if you're planning to do consulting or give speeches. Your bio should be in prose. No poetry, no iambic pentameter, no bullets. Include the same photo that's on your LinkedIn profile.

Photo. Photos are important, so upload a couple of good headshots of you in professional clothing. Color, smiling, wearing business or business/casual clothes. Have a nice haircut. Guys, try to avoid facial hair—especially in conservative environments. Gals, wear a little make-up. No bar scenes with you holding a drink, looking goofy, or making out with your boy- or girl-friend. This is serious business. Mike, a smart, talented client, actually had a job offer rescinded after his prospective employer saw some objectionable pics on Mike's Facebook page.

Personalized URL. An absolute must-have, so people can easily find you. Edit your profile URL so it's www.linkedin. com/pub/in/yourname with no numbers or slashes after your name That's the name of the game. You may want to set up your own website if you are considering consulting and would like someplace to showcase your writing samples, research, photos and so on.

A single phone number where you can always be reached. I recommend the cell phone that you carry 24/7. Record your outgoing message in your own voice and simply state that you're not able to talk right now, but that you'll call back as soon as you can. Your voice should be strong, confident, calm, and upbeat. Speak slowly and clearly and say, "Hello," not "Hi." Don't sing or rap, and make sure you don't accidentally (or deliberately) record traffic noise, barking dogs, or your kids shouting in the background. Your outgoing message may be a prospective employer's first contact with you, and it needs to make a positive, lasting impression. Finally, set your voicemail to pick up after no more than three rings. More than that and people may just give up and move on to the next resume in their pile.

A few words about phone etiquette: If your phone rings and you're not able to have a decent conversation, try to answer it anyway and tell the caller that you'll call back at a time that's good for them. That said, do *not* answer the phone if you're in the restroom. (I know, you can't believe I'm actually giving this advice, but trust me …) If possible, explain why you can't talk—you're sitting in a dentist's chair, coaching your daughter's volleyball team, etc. That's less likely to make people feel that you're blowing them off to do something that's more important than speaking with them.

Advisory Board. Staying around positive people is a must. And being with positive people who know you and support you is ideal. Think about asking three or four people whom you trust to be your informal Advisory Board. You can get their advice, bounce ideas off them, review your action plan, and be around "positive speak." Meet with them periodically, face-to-face. And bring them a dead mouse! Could be flowers, chocolates, pretty stamps, note cards, or just some info. But don't go empty-handed. Remember: optimism is a key to success.

Okay, I know you're anxious to get out there and start setting up meetings. And you're almost there. But before you can pick up the phone, there's one more thing we need to do: make sure that the product you're trying to sell—you—looks, sounds, and acts as well as it possibly can. Ready for the next step?

Chapter 4

Managing Your Presence

First impressions are almost always the longest-lasting impressions—and you get only one chance to make one. That's why you should always—and I do mean *always*—be first-impression-ready. Think of it as the Power of Ten: The critical components of your first impression are the first ten seconds people lay eyes on you, the first ten steps you take toward them, and the first ten words out of your mouth.

Despite all that stuff people say about not judging a book by its cover, the fact is that people (and by "people," I mean "anyone who's in a position to hire you") do exactly that every day. My client, Edgar, is a great example. Edgar dressed impeccably every day, no matter where he went. And one day, that really paid off. When a recruiter contacted us and asked for a CPA, I immediately started calling clients. Edgar wasn't at the very top of my list, but the first two said they needed to go home to get changed before they could make the meeting and the third candidate didn't answer her cell phone. But the recruiter needed the CPA yesterday. Edgar was ready to roll, got the meeting—and the job.

Scott was having coffee with a person he had been introduced to via email, by a former colleague. Coincidentally, Scott was meeting with me first. When I saw him in his slacks and shirt, I asked if he had hung up the suit jacket in the office closet. When he looked perplexed, I explained that a suit and tie was appropriate attire for all meetings. You don't know who these people are, who they know, or whether they themselves are hiring managers. Make a great first impression at all times, and that it begins with what you're wearing to that first meeting. When in doubt, overdress. Better that than underdressed. My client, Brian, had 185 "coffees" and was in a suit for all of them. He eventually landed a great job. You don't get a chance to do these meetings over. Once it doesn't go well, it's all over. Anything we can do to build relationships and have meetings go well, is something we should be doing.

I'm sure you've heard the expression, "dress for success." But what, exactly, does that mean? Well, to start with, "dressing" involves a lot more than just clothes. The "cover" people are so carefully judging includes your posture, how you walk, how you talk (vocabulary, loudness, softness, level of confidence, intonation, speed), and, of course, your personal hygiene.

Ultimately, the success or failure of your dress will depend on the industry sector and the culture of the organization you're trying to fit in with. What works in New York probably won't work in Japan, and might not even fly in Chicago. It also depends on how well you know the person you're interacting with. Never forget, though, that except in very rare circumstances, people you're meeting with are *not* your friends—and don't let yourself get lulled into thinking they are.

When interviewing, networking, or having an informational meeting, please remember to keep buttoned up and professional at all times. Don't get comfortable, slouch, or use slang (unless it's industry specific). This is work, not play, and these people are not your friends. Full battle dress, guard up. Even if it's just an informational interview or networking meeting, every meeting is important and you should consider them potential interviews. Ask good questions, have attentive body language and a smile. Be cognizant and respectful of their time and make the time with you interesting and enjoyable. People hire people they like. Would the person you're talking with want to sit next to you on the red eye back from the West Coast? If not, you may not be making your best impression. Always be professional, poised, and deferential. Always. That said, there are a few general ground rules that I advise you to keep in mind at all times.

Look young. Unfortunately, despite the fact that it's illegal for employers to discriminate on the basis of age, it's harder to find a job if you're over 40—even more so if you're over 50.

Act young, too, but don't go overboard. Have presence and energy but don't over-use slang or get "casual" at a meeting.

Be nice—to everyone. That means the security guards in the parking lot, the receptionist, the assistant. You may not be interviewing with them, but believe me, if you treat them badly, the person you are interviewing with will hear about it. You just don't know who they are, whom they're related to, and whose ear they've got.

A classic, well-fitting suit made from a nice fabric is always in style. Crisp is good, and if your slacks or shirt are supposed to have creases, make sure they do. Go with a white or blue shirt and a non-neon silk tie in the red or blue family. Red is a conservative color and blue shirts tend to make men look younger. Try to mimic the dress code of the firm you are going to. Look at their websites, annual reports and podcasts to see what the leaders and staff wear.

For men, the hair should be relatively short. For women, contemporary and chic—and watch the color and roots.

For men, a clean-shaven look is best, unless you're up for a "hip" or "creative" job where stubble is common. Otherwise, facial hair tends to make men look older, so avoid it in any conservative environment (unless you look like you're 17 and need to put on a few years).

For women, less is usually more. Wear simple makeup—lipstick, mascara, and blush—and simple accessories, like one ring, post earrings and a simple chain, scarf, or pin. Keep it professional—statement jewelry can be lovely, but may send the wrong message in a conservative environment, so limit yourself to one piece. Carry only one bag and make sure you pack it with nothing more than essentials. Bulges are definitely out. Remember, some color is important, so don't go all black. Memorable is hire-able.

Always wear a watch. No, not a Mickey Mouse, and leave the fake (or the real) Rolex at home.

Shine your shoes and make sure they don't look run-down. Gentlemen, be sure to check the heels of your shoes *and* your socks.

Brush your teeth and carry mints. I shouldn't have to tell you that, but you'd be amazed at how many people don't get it. You may find yourself in pretty close quarters with others, and the last thing you want them to be thinking about is how to end the interview and get a breath of fresh air. Oh, and floss is your friend. Enough said.

Take a picture of yourself dressed for a job interview or important networking meeting. Ask three trusted people (hello Advisory Board!) to give you some honest feedback. And take a good, long look at yourself in a full-length mirror. Turn all the way 'round. Look sideways and in the back. Do you look perfect? I still picture myself as 29 and a size 8 ...

When meeting with people, be enthusiastic but not frenetic, engaged without seeming desperate. And above all, come across as knowledgeable about technology and social media. If you aren't already, spend some time getting yourself up to speed. Joking about how you're a technophobe or reminiscing about mimeographing or faxing on thermal paper isn't funny. And it pegs you as hopelessly out-of-date.

One way to fight ageism is to talk technology. Don't be afraid to mention your Facebook page or LinkedIn profile (again, just be sure it's at least 90 percent complete). If you blog or tweet, say so (assuming it's safe for public consumption). Know what Tumblr is. My client, Will's, passion for baseball helped him land a job after a prospective manager stumbled onto Will's blog.

Show that you're flexible and open to new things. If you're taking a challenging class or just got back from a hiking trip, talk about it (but you might want to skip over the month-long African safari or the trek up Everest—you risk coming across as wealthy or entitled, qualities that employers generally aren't looking for). Don't talk about every book you read—we all read so there's nothing terribly special about that—unless you can discuss a great, non-business book you think your audience would be interested in.

Conquering Your Obstacles So You Can Get Hired

Everyone has an obstacle (or two or three or more) that may keep them from getting hired. Knowing what yours are and solving them is very important in this process—and very hard to do. For example, is it your age (or the age you look?) The fact that you are not an agile learner? In a world where we are all being asked to do more with less, you've got to be flexible and wear a lot of hats. Have no real subject matter expertise? One of the key elements in your job search is learning how to build rapport with all types of people. My client Maura told me how she thought that looking for a job was a lot like speed dating. I agree! You meet a ton of folks, most of whom you're not going to marry (or even have a second date with), but you must meet them, make a good impression, learn about them. Whether they're your next hiring manager or not, you'll at least have them in your Rolodex and as LinkedIn contacts. Job search is about being uncomfortable. What could be less comfortable than a first date when you have no idea who you're meeting? As I've said, it's a numbers game. But it's also a quality game, meaning that it's better to have ten meetings than five, but better still to have five good ones than ten bad ones. You control this! Smile, use their name, have mutual interest points, and be authentic and warm. They have to LIKE you! Remember to ask a question or two about them. Thanks to the Internet, there's no excuse for not doing your homework and stalking them (a tad).

Here's a list of obstacles I see fairly frequently. In some cases, the client is aware of their obstacle. In other cases, they have no idea. As you read through this list (which is by no means exhaustive) do a little honest soul searching. It's best to identify—and learn to overcome—any obstacles you may have before you start setting up meetings and interviews.

Not knowing you have one

Your age

Negative speak

Bad body language

Lack of skills

Lack of technology

Poor references

Overpaid

Underpaid

Same firm for years and years

Overtalker

Extremely nervous

Bad reputation

Short stints

Shy/introvert

Low energy

Bankruptcy or bad background check possible

Arrogant/know it all personality

Poor communication skills

Poor test taking skills

Poor interviewing skills

Inability to build rapport

Poor closings

No strategic follow up

Same firm for 15 years

As I've said, there are very few do-overs in the job search world. People are too busy for you to call them back and say, "Okay, I did that really poorly...." "Can I send you a new resume?" "Would you mind introducing me to your boss again?" I think not. So be sure to do your homework about the individual and the company you're meeting with—both online and in person if possible. And take as much time as you need to get your look, your pitch, your voice, and everything else in top shape *before* you walk into that meeting. You'll be glad you did.

Notes

Chapter 5

Your Job Search Action Plan

Tom had the best job search action plan I had ever seen. On the first page, he identified his job functions, where he had worked, what his accomplishments were, and included clear examples of his differentiation. On the second page, he included information on some community service projects he was involved in, and his interest in sports—great conversation starters—along with a list of the sectors and firms within those sectors where he would like to work. With his action plan and verbal positioning all set, Tom was able to use them as a roadmap for his successful job search. Jill went one step further and included one or two examples with the functions that strengthened her cause, positioning and pitch.

One of the most important components of your job search action plan is a comprehensive list, similar to the one Tom put together, of companies you'd like to reach. As we discussed earlier, it's important to understand your strengths, your skill sets, how you can actually help your potential employer, your value proposition or USP (unique selling proposition), and your personal brand. Using that as a base, you'll start thinking about companies where the unique package you have to offer (you, of course) would best fit. Having this in mind will give you a jumping off point.

Start by putting together the names of companies that are similar to the one you just came out of. Write down some of the ancillary firms that provide services to that sector, smaller companies in the same category, privately held ones, or private equity firms that have your type of company in their portfolio. Perhaps your previous clients and customers might be potential targets for you.

Keep in mind, though, that your list isn't (and should never be) set in concrete. Some of the options you're interested in will disappear, while new ones will open up. Don't let this throw you. As long as your list has more than ten companies on it at a time, you're okay. Your ability to roll with the tide while keeping a positive outlook and optimistic attitude will separate you from the mob of disgruntled, dissatisfied, disenfranchised job hunters who are competing with you for the same jobs.

And don't rule out the possibility of a complete career shift. One client, Bernie, left an operations job to open a franchise, Richard went from a financial services firm to a hospital, and Beth left a sales job to go to nursing school. As long as you know what you're good at and what motivates you (all part of the Inventory we talked about in Chapter 1), you may discover other areas where your skills are applicable. All you need to learn is what's possible. Then add that information to your action plan options. Do read "What Color is Your Parachute" as it is very helpful and is revised often.

The exercise of writing out your action plan will help you stay focused by keeping your list of target companies and individuals in front of you at all times. That's important, because given that it often takes forever to set up meetings, following your plan will allow you to pursue multiple goals at the same time, and will help identify what your most logical next steps should be. A simple spreadsheet also helps you track your job search. You don't want to drop any balls or forget to follow-through on a lead someone gives you. If you do get a referral, be sure to make contact that person within 48 hours of getting their information, and get back to the person who gave you the lead and let them know how it all turned out. They will so appreciate you circling back to them. It is again, all about how you make others feel.

Using Your Job Search Action Plan

As we discussed in Chapter 3, you should *not* pull out your resume in an informational or networking meeting. You don't want your target to switch to "I've-got-to-get-this-guy/gal-out-of-my-office" mode. But *do* talk about your action plan. The person you're meeting with might have contacts at one or more of the firms on your target list, or better yet, contacts at a company you never even thought of. If you're using your action plan as a conversation starter, your target may also be able to give you some valuable advice about better ways to highlight your skills, and even how to add in skills you hadn't thought to include in the plan.

If you can smoothly fit it into the conversation, ask if there is anyone else at the firm that they would feel comfortable introducing you to for informational purposes only. You're trying to build a campaign within the firm even though there is officially no role. Companies create new roles all the time when they come across the right candidate: *you*! However, try not to talk too much about other firms or ask for referrals to other people until you're completely sure that the company you're meeting with isn't interested in you.

One last thought: at networking meetings, informational interviews and formal interviews, people ask questions that they hope will elicit telling truths about yourself. They're trying to see if you are negative and bitter, or honest, a team player, and a good fit with their organization. Be careful! For example, "You sound like you did a great job with that project. Why didn't they keep you on after the merger?" This speaks to your ability to not get defensive or speak negatively about your former employer or bosses. Detox before you embark on looking for that new or better job. People can see through bad karma, even when you think you're hiding it well. Or, "What is your number one weakness?" This is looking for someone who is a grown-up and self-aware and knows he or she is not perfect and is willing to admit it. This is where you might say, "I'm very focused on the details and sometimes I need to step back to see the forest instead of just the trees or "I'm sometimes impatient, but I know it all needs to be a collaborative effort and I'm working hard on breathing in and out and not snapping or sighing at anyone." This tells them you can be picky, but also that you're trying to mitigate it and overcome your weakness. Or they might ask "What would your subordinates (or your peers or your boss) say about you?" This is about your operating style. Are you a role model, a mentor, a collaborative worker? A good answer is, "They'd say I'm a great leader who works hard to give credit to everyone else on the team and focuses on results *and* professional development." Try your action plan out on your network that knows you first and get some valuable feedback and suggestions. I remember bringing mine to a networking lunch with my old boss and he said, you are missing the one great thing about you—your uncanny ability to bring out the best in others. I quickly added that attribute.

Notes

Chapter 6

Network or Not Work
(or, Bring a Dead Mouse)

At last! Francine was finally meeting the hiring manager she'd been trying to see for months. On previous calls, he'd mentioned his love for poker, and had even invited her to join his game (she declined, as she plays poorly!). Before their face-to-face meeting, she purchased a small set of poker chips and presented them to the manager. Memorable? You bet. And remember, memorable is hire-able.

Somewhere along the way, networking got a dirty name. Let's understand that networking is merely speaking with another person and building rapport. In this chapter, the goal is to help you construct the road that will ultimately lead to getting hired. Don't worry, we'll start traveling down that road soon. Right now, though, we're focusing on networking, which is about building reciprocal long-lasting relationships, *not* asking people for a job. More than 75 percent of my clients landed jobs through networking. Not sitting online, not posting their resume, not relying on others or search firms, and certainly not applying for roles online.

Since the majority of all jobs aren't posted, odds are that you'll find your next position (and probably the one after that) through your network—*not* through job postings or ads. Many of the jobs posted have actually already been filled; but no one has taken the time to remove the posting. Or they have an internal candidate already slated for that role. And there is no beating an internal candidate. With companies unable to provide the high salaries or perks they could in the past, they are doing all they can to keep their top talent. So if a high performer sees an opening they want, they can normally obtain it over an outsider. There is this wonderful "hidden" job market where there is work to be done but no headcount approved. Remember, "no" really means "not now," so stay in touch! Companies are always looking for good talent. And when they find it, they somehow miraculously find the money to hire that terrific athlete too.

Actually, in most cases, the people in your direct network won't have a job for you. What they *do* have, though, is even more important: networks of their own. The math is pretty simple: Having ten people in your network is great. But if each of those 10 has his or her own network of ten, you're already up to 100 possible connections. And if each of those 100 has a 10-person network, you're up to 1,000 in no time. In my experience, the connection that leads to the job is usually between three and six degrees of separation from you. Don't have a network yet? Well, you'd better get cracking. Sara had 367 face to face meetings with her network and her network's network in order to land her perfect job.

When you're looking for a job, there's no need to suffer in silence. The more people who know, the better your chances of finding what you're looking for. People want to help, so let them! Start with your family, in-laws, friends, neighbors, people from your place of worship, parents of your kids' friends (you'll make a lot more connections on the sidelines of a soccer field than on a golf course). Reach out to colleagues and bosses from all of your previous jobs, not just the most recent ones—people who "grew up" with you professionally—and don't forget about vendors, suppliers, and clients you may have worked with in the past. Ask these people whom they know, and for referrals to others they respect, admire, or think might be open to a conversation with you.

And don't prejudge your network. Contact everyone— everyone knows someone, and it never hurts to ask. Ask for the contact or referral and then say yes to meetings. You just never know. If someone says, "I can introduce you to ... . Would that be helpful?" Say yes. That person undoubtedly has a network so you can then go further afield away from your initial network circle.

There are lots of other ways to build your network. For example, check out alumni organizations (high school, college, and grad school), join an adult sports league, start going to meetings and conferences put on by professional associations and trade groups. See if you can sign on to be a speaker or panelist, introduce the speakers or panelists, or ask the organizers about volunteering. There are also dozens of groups that cross business sector lines. Some are organized by functionality (Risk Management Association, Financial Managers Association, International Association of Business Communicators, FEI, MENG. TENG, FENG (marketing/technology and financial executives networking group), gender (FWA, 85 Broads, 100 Women in Hedge Funds, New York Women in Media and Television, etc.), ethnicity (100 Black Men, Asian American Federation, the Diversity Consortium, etc.), volunteerism (Kiwanis, Rotary, etc.), educational institutions (alumni associations, Phi Beta Kappa chapters, etc.), or even geographical location. Volunteer at a not-for-profit and meet other volunteers, staff and the Board. Add them to your networking list. You should by now have quite a healthy list of people that you know from a myriad of sources. The list will grow and change. Ask for referrals and add those (don't forget to send them LinkedIn invites when appropriate) to your networking list. I don't connect to strangers or people I have never met or spoken with, but I had one client who connected with over 800 strangers. To each his own but I like to know my network and feel comfortable that when someone says, "would you please introduce me to Diana?" I know whom they are talking about.

Networking, Step by Step

"Networking" is one of those words that we've all heard—and think we understand. But in my experience, it's more than just a word, or even a concept. Instead, it's a methodical, five-step process.

1. Identify the target

2. Contact the target

3. Do your research

4. Have the meeting

5. Follow up tenaciously

Let's take a look at each of these steps in detail.

1. Identify the Target

Now that you have a pretty good handle on your network, put together a list of every company that you might like to work for. Does anyone you know or worked with in the past work there now? Used to work there? Does anyone in your *network* know someone who works or used to work there? As I mentioned above, the majority of jobs aren't posted, so networking is the best way of finding out what's out there. It's a whole hidden job market. So send emails out and *ask*.

Some people are natural networkers—they always seem to be making personal and professional connections. At one point, my client, Carolyn, had 64 networking meetings in *one week*, and Justin had 167 in just a few months! Granted, most of these took place at networking events where there were a lot of people to meet with, but but Carolyn and Justin thrive in reaching out to strangers.

Unfortunately, most of us are far from natural networkers. As with so much else in life, it's more about quality than quantity. Sure, having five to seven face-to-face meetings every week is great—if you can do it. But even if you have only two or three, try to make each one as productive and fruitful as possible. Never go without thinking through the agenda. When you were working, did you put together a meeting without an agenda? I think not!

2. Contact the Target

When trying to set up a meeting, don't try to reach the referral directly unless you absolutely have to. Having your contact (or your contact's contact) make the introduction is a much more powerful way to go in than your making a cold call and saying, "Hi, I was referred by Sue Smith. Do you have time next Tuesday?" However, as soon as the initial introduction has been made, make contact yourself right away. In most cases, you'll start with a quick email and then follow up with a phone call. But find out your target's preferred mode of communication and do it that way—*not* what's easiest for you.

Email is *not* ideal. It's passive and we all get hundreds of them every day. If there's no alternative, at least be sure to put something meaningful into the subject line—such as the name of the person who made the referral. Hopefully, that will keep your emails out of your target's SPAM box. Do *not* send your resume. Send your bullets. Nothing is more of a door-closer than sending your resume. People sometimes feel that you are asking them for a job, not a networking meeting. Be clear you are not asking for a job.

Be pleasantly persistent and tenacious, but don't stalk. If you've tried three times (twice by email and once by phone) but haven't had any luck getting on your target's calendar, circle back with your initial contact. Understand that delays happen. It's easy to take someone's lack of responsiveness as a personal rejection, but it usually isn't. They're just busy doing their job. After three weeks of getting absolutely nowhere with what had sounded like a really promising contact, my client Grant was getting frustrated and a little depressed. But after getting back in touch with the contact who had made the introduction, he found out that the woman he was trying to meet had been nursing her ailing husband.

Chances are, you're reaching out to people with busy jobs who are being asked to pack even more work (including meeting with you) into what was already a pretty crazy schedule. Remember when you were working? How many times did you let that outreach or networking call or email slip to the next day, the day after that, or drop altogether? You didn't do it out of spite, you were just plain busy.

Do not show your annoyance in emails or phone calls; try to relax and remember that job hunting is a numbers game. Keep sending emails and making those calls, and you'll probably get six out of ten meetings. Some of them might be only a five-minute phone call, but, hey, any incremental progress counts, and remember to invite these folks (when you think they'll be comfortable) via LinkedIn. One way to figure out if you should invite someone into your LinkedIn it to ask yourself if you would be comfortable introducing them to your network. If not, take a pass.

Cutting the Cord

If the person you're reaching out to has never been unem-ployed or doesn't know anyone who has been, he or she may be slow to help or respond. They just don't "get it." After trying seven times (four emails and three phone calls) to get someone to speak with you or meet with you, and it doesn't happen, it's time to cut the cord. But do it actively, by sending a final email that says: "So sorry we were never able to connect or speak. All good wishes for a terrific year. Best regards, Steve"

There are three reasons to do this. First, you've been thinking that you have something going but you actually don't. So you might as well free up the space in your heart and brain and start focusing on a meeting that might truly happen. Second, it empowers you. Sometimes in a job search, you feel a tad like a victim, quite vulnerable and with no control over anything. Taking the initiative and ending things puts you in the driver's seat. Third, it sometimes gets people to respond. Guilt can be a won-derful motivator! Just remember to always be polite, persistent, and nice. What goes around comes around … Always try to pay it forward. The reality is, if you live long enough, you'll see all kinds of neat stuff. There are several people I know from the business who actually ruined their chances of another job in our business, lost their marriages and wonderful family lives or served jail time. What goes around, comes around. Focus on being the very best you can be, Don't just do your best. Do what is necessary to get it done. Always remember to ask yourself the most important question … how did I make them feel?

3. Do Your Research

Okay, you've got the meeting. Now what? Well, first congratulate yourself on completing the hardest part of the process! Next, start researching and doing due diligence about the person you're meeting with, the firm, and their business sector. Google is a good place to start, but don't end there. You can find a lot of great financial information on sites like Yahoo! Finance, Schwab, Vanguard, Bloomberg, and Motley Fool. Spend some time on the company's website, reading everything you can. For public companies, read the CEO's letter to shareholders (you'll find it in the company's annual report). Generally, in these communiqués, the CEO shares strategic plans for the coming fiscal year and will talk about the company's culture—very important background knowledge for your face-to-face meetings. Pull up the company's three most recent press releases so you're up on the latest developments.

Speak to people who have worked there, work there now, or who know the firm and its culture and products. The day of the interview, re-Google them and read up on any last-minute news stories. One client, Theresa, told me how she found out—while sitting on the train on the way to a meeting—that the company had just announced a major acquisition. Definitely good information to have. Steve told of an interviewer asking specifically about something that was on the front page of the newspaper that morning. Unfortunately, Steve hadn't read the paper that day! Remember to use social networking sites to learn more about your targets: associations they belong to, children they have, universities they attended, panels they've spoken on, articles they've written, and so on.

4. Have the Meeting

Once you get a meeting, it's critical to keep in mind that you're not there to talk about yourself or to ask for a job. In fact, the *worst* thing you can do is come right out and ask, "Do you have anything for me?" I know that this is a paradigm shift for most job seekers. After all, you do want a job, right? And it's tempting to talk about yourself, your accomplishments, and how perfect you'd be for the company. But don't. For now, all you're doing is building bridges and listening. Lots of listening. As a rule, spend 80 percent of your time using your ears, 20 percent using your mouth. The more you know about the people you're meeting with and the circles they run in, the more likely you'll be able to make a specific request later. People hire people they like—and who like them. By listening carefully, you're saying, "I get you, I like you, I'm interested in what you have to say and what you represent." My client Don met several people at the firm he was interested in and each of them passed him on to yet another person at the same firm. Soon, he had his "village" of champions inside that firm and was offered a job! Campaign for what you want at firms that make sense for you. Don't worry if there is a role open. They will open one for you.

There are three components to every networking meeting:

◊ The Give

◊ The Get

◊ The Get Out (next steps)

The Give is your gift to the person you're seeing—the famous dead mouse that's in the title of this book (and the title of this chapter). No one gave more dead mice than my client, Chuck. Which is why he landed a terrific position in only 60 days—the only client I've ever had who found a job that quickly (remember, the average for senior execs is over 10 months). He helped more people in more ways than I can enumerate. If he saw a job online that he thought was a good fit for someone else, he sent it to that person; he sponsored people who wanted to be part of networking forums he was in or groups he belonged to; he connected people he thought would be useful and helpful to each other. If he wasn't the right guy for the job they were speaking about, he gave them names and numbers of people who were. Dead mice galore.

After the initial ice breakers, you present your dead mouse. My client Pooja once brought a small baby gift to a potential hiring manager that she had met with several times. Remember, it's how you make them feel that counts. When you bring someone a gift that lets them know you're thinking of them, they, in turn, will think of you. It's human nature to reciprocate. You start, and whoever gets your gift will follow.

I spend about half my practice strategizing with clients about dead mice—how to identify them and present them without looking contrived. It doesn't have to be (and shouldn't be) anything big or expensive. It just needs to be thoughtful. Say, for example, you've got a meeting with a gal who's just about to send her oldest child off to college. If you've been in that spot yourself, a book, an article, or even some advice from a pro could be in order. My client,

Dan, had read a great book about dads and daughters that he shared with many others during his job search. He even got the book signed by the author. Or maybe you know the person you're meeting with is a Jets fan, and you bring an autographed cap.

Your dead mouse doesn't always have to be an actual object. One client, Joe, heard that a mutual colleague had recently changed jobs, and he passed that info along to the target, who was delighted to hear about his friend. That seemingly simple piece of information also gave the target the very clear message that Joe was a guy who's keeping up on the industry and its players. Another client, Rich, would identify other job seekers to a company if he wasn't the right fit. That established him as someone who was well-connected and cared enough about the company's success to refer good people to them.

The point here is that you're trying to differentiate yourself in a market where there are many, many more candidates than jobs. If you're not sure how to find appropriate dead mice, you can always set up Google Alerts which will send you any information that shows up on the web that mentions your target, companies you're looking into, business trends, and any other items of interest. Not coming into a meeting empty handed can set the tone for the rest of the meeting and make the difference between an okay meeting and a truly stellar one. Put your target first, not yourself. What can you do to be helpful professionally or personally, so that you'll be seen as a resource? The key is to be absolutely authentic. If you're not, folks will know, and you'll be worse off than if you hadn't brought anything at all.

Scott met with a ton of folks asking for a role, job, or opportunity. But it wasn't until he started coming up with ideas of ways that he could help people, that he began to get assignments—and then a job! Be creative and thoughtful—what can you do to be an extra pair of hands? What could they use you for now? Make a role for yourself. Never assume that other people will do it for you. The key is to be absolutely authentic. If you're not, folks will know, and you'll be worse off than if you hadn't brought anything at all.

The Get is what you're asking for. Let's say the company you're meeting with is in the consumer package industry, and there are four companies you've identified that you'd like to speak with. Could your target introduce you to anyone at those companies? Not necessarily about a job, just to see what areas are growing and where the trends are. Remember, whether networking or in an interview, if the person is busy scribbling notes down on paper, they have disengaged from you. Stop talking, ask a question and reel them back in. Watch your body language, smile, use their names, and go back to a part of the conversation where he/she was engaged. Rewind in essence. Begin to figure out how to cut the meeting short and make a graceful and intelligent exit.

The Get Out comes toward the end of the meeting and is simply a way of keeping the conversation going. This could be giving the target a card, getting one of hers (try to get a business card from everyone you meet with, so you'll have their title, address, and correct spelling of their name—you'll need all that for your thank-you notes), or asking for a time when you should check back to see whether she was able to make the introductions you'd talked about. Also ask whether she prefers a phone call or email. Have a very solid closing; it's how you're remembered. The key to all of this is to make your pitch during the meeting. Coming up with an idea and emailing it in two days afterwards will have little effect. Too little, too late. Look for those opportunities and be ready to ask, "Would that be helpful? I'd love to do it and it should only take four days' worth of work and six or seven meetings with your staff ..." Give the idea or intellectual capital and get the work. Give to Get.

Remember that many of the people you meet with are too overworked and overwhelmed to either think about adding headcount or come up with a project or an assignment for you. They barely have enough hours in the day to get their jobs done and get home at a decent hour to be with their families. In cases like this—when there doesn't seem to be a clear job for you—you need to think about how you're going to create value for them. For example, you meet a business manager who tells you she's having trouble getting all of her projects done on time and on budget. And as a seasoned project manager, you know all it takes is some workflow analysis and a methodology that fits with the company's work and platform. Offer to have a few conversations with her team and then put together an action plan they can implement. You'll include the timing, cost, and resources the manager will need to get the project done quickly and seamlessly, without disrupting the current work or making anyone uneasy with all of your questions (or your mere presence).

5. Follow up Tenaciously

My mom always told me that I was brought up, not dug up—so act accordingly.

Within 24 hours after your meeting, be sure to send an email thank-you to the person you met with—if you met with 11, send out 11. If you're in doubt about whether to send a thank-you, send one. No one ever didn't get a job because she thanked too many people. On the other hand, there are plenty of people who didn't get jobs because they didn't send notes, which made them come across as rude. Keep in mind that we're talking about thank-*you* notes, not notes about you, how wonderful you are, and how perfect you are for the job. Do not send joint or group emails; individualize and personalize them.

Be sure to send *handwritten* thank-you's to the people who went to bat for you and set up the meeting. You may need to keep in touch with them in case you need their help with future follow-through. In the meantime, get ready for your next meeting—and don't forget your dead mouse.

Notes

Chapter 7

Activity vs. Productivity

You used to wake up in the morning and go to work, now you just wake up. But remember the long hours you used to put into your job at the office? This is no time for slacking off. This isn't a vacation or a time to catch up on all of those chores you're behind on. If you really need to get things done around the house—and you can afford it—consider taking a month off to adjust to having lost your job and to take care of all those non-job-related things. Whether it's re-connecting with your family, going to visit your parents, taking French classes, or going on vacation, do it! Then you can jump in renewed and refreshed, and focus completely on your new, full-time occupation: finding work.

When you're in the midst of a full-blown job search, there are a million things to do. Make calls, send emails, go to networking conferences, check out job fairs, reach out to people who have been referred to you, work on and post your resume, get your LinkedIn profile perfect, and keep your tracking sheets up to date. As we've discussed, it's taking most people longer to find a job these days than ever, so it's crucial that you use your time wisely. Right below this paragraph you'll find a chart with my suggestion for how to divide and categorize your efforts—in general terms. Take a look at it, and then I'll show you what a typical job search schedule might look like.

A few clarifications:

Face-to-face meetings. This includes networking, informational, or any other meeting that gets you out of your pajamas and out from behind your computer screen. As you spend more time on your job search, the face-to-face percentage should grow to about 75 percent of your time, with research, emails, and phone calls taking up the remaining 25 percent.

Research. Thinking through your target companies, knowing a lot about the firms and people you are going to see, understanding which industry sectors are growing or at least healthy.

Communications. Emailing, calling, inviting LinkedIn friends, thank you notes, sending interesting articles.

Job postings, headhunters, and recruiters. Applying for positions, reaching out to five or six headhunters/recruiters. It's best if you can be introduced to these headhunters by someone who knows them.

Structure your job-hunting work day in a very similar way to how you might have structured your on-the-job work day. My client, Sandy, was at his desk every morning, wearing a suit and tie, at exactly 8:30. And I'm talking about when he was unemployed. Sandy took his job-hunting very seriously, and he spent his days meticulously hitting the phones, writing cover letters, sending emails, and setting up face-to-face meetings. On page 67 is an example of what a typical job-hunting daily schedule might look like.

It's very easy to fall into the trap of networking, making calls, and setting up meetings because you want to keep busy—and you want everyone to know that you're looking for a job. But there's a big difference between being truly productive and simply spinning your wheels. Here are some tips that will help you keep your job search focused, organized, and disciplined:

1. Touch each piece of paper only once. Don't just move it around from place to place. Either deal with it immediately or file it away.

2. Make up your business cards once. Send the draft to two people you trust (career coach and friend who works in the business sector you are pursuing) and get their comments. *Then* have the cards printed.

3. Send impactful, actionable emails so you'll get replies and answers the first time you reach out. Show one to someone on your Advisory Board and then you will have a template for your search going forward. For example:

Subject: Quick catch-up?

Good morning Brian,
Hope you are well and had a great New Year's holiday. I ran into Arun who sends his regards. Sorry I've been out of touch; would you have time for a quick catch-up call or coffee?

Thanks and best,
Charlotte
(555) 555-5555

---

4. Leave detailed voicemail messages—including a concise heads-up about why you're calling—so you can avoid endless rounds of telephone tag.

5. Track your job search to ensure your metrics are holding (Are you making your target of 5–10 calls every day? Seven face-to-face meetings every week?). But don't spend too much time focusing on systems and complicated processes that take a lot of time and energy to complete. A simple Excel spreadsheet or alphabetical listing by target, company, and/or name of contact, is just fine. The easier it is to update, the more likely you'll actually use it. One of the most important reasons to have

a good tracking system is so that 30 people later, you still know how you got that contact and that job. And can thank everyone along the way.

My Schedule for Today

7:00 am – 8:00 am	Wake up and work out (walk, run, swim, weights, yoga, meditate)
8:00 am – 8:30 am	Shower, breakfast, get dressed
8:30 am–10:30 am	Turn on phone, return calls, check emails and return those (be sure to carefully review your emails before clicking Send)
10:30 am – 11:30 am	Stand up, have tea, stretch, call a friend or someone from your Advisory Board*
11:00 am – 11:30 am	Change into "work clothes" and head off to your lunch/ networking meeting
11:30 am -1:30 pm	Travel to your meeting, have your meeting, come home
1:30 pm–5:30 pm	Send a thank you note to your lunch partner, apply for one job online, send seven LinkedIn invites, answer emails, call four people to set up meetings for next week, research for your next meeting (interview, informational, etc.)**

*More about your Advisory Board in Chapter 3.
** Never schedule two meetings back-to-back. The first one may start late or run long, or you might get asked to meet more people or join them for lunch or a drink.

6. Be careful that you're not scheduling meetings just for the sake of having meetings. Go through your calendar and make sure that each meeting has a purpose and agenda. If it doesn't, make it a phone call instead. If it still looks like it might fall flat, put it off altogether by telling the person you're meeting with (or calling) that you're finishing up your job search marketing plan and would like to circle back when it's done. That should give you at least a month. Everyone is overbooked these days, and if they can take one meeting off their calendar without feeling guilty about blowing *you* off, they'll be thrilled.

7. One of the best ways to ensure that you're always moving forward is to write your target companies down and give yourself a deadline of 60 days to have had conversations with all of them. Triangulate if at all possible: have a stronghold in the target company that is your initial contact, but add two others in the organization who can advocate for you. The ideal is three advocates inside and three from the outside calling your "insiders" over a period of time … not all in one week. If at all possible, one of those insiders would be in HR, while the other two would be in the actual business lines (meaning non-HR positions).

8. Meet with someone on your Advisory Board twice a month to keep your feet to the fire and ensure you're keeping to your schedule. Then update your list to cross off contacts you've connected with and

add new targets. Seek and embrace feedback. Ask how you are perceived. Ask for advice on how to be more helpful, value-added, and current in this ever-changing market environment.

9. Be sure to build some "me time" into your day. You need to arrive at every meeting looking and feeling your very best. So whether it's the gym in the morning, a midday walk, or an evening swim, do whatever keeps you of sound mind *and* body. Our stress shows on our face and on our bodies.

Notes

Chapter 8

Don't Fall in Love

During the job-hunting process, you're going to meet a ton of people and have interviews at a number of organizations. I know it's hard, but it's important to try not to fall in love with any of them (I'm talking about the companies, not the people—although falling in love with the people probably isn't a very good idea either). Austin spent three months focused on one specific financial services firm. But one day he found out that the person whose job he was hoping to take over had decided *not* to leave the company after all. Poof! In a nanosecond, Austin's perfect job disappeared. Mike spent 2 ½ months on one job with a large firm and they ended up hiring the other guy. Don't fall in love with one job that you do not have. Keep all the balls in the air and all your networking meetings continuing onward.

And Rich was convinced that Big Bank was going to hire him. They asked all the right questions (when can you start?) and said all the right things (we really need you here—you'll fit in perfectly . . .) but they didn't. Fortunately, Rich kept a few other balls in the air, and a smaller, but more-profitable investment bank hired him a few weeks later. The moral of the story is: Finish all your meetings and processes and don't let anything drop until you start your new job. After that, you might go back to your old habits (I hope not) but at least until then, you will meet with lots of folks, practice your pitch, improve your presentation, and adjust your style for many different audiences.

Until you've got a signed employment letter in hand, or you've got your new office key and are ordering business cards and hiring an assistant, keep your options open. How many? In my experience, five is a good number. It's nice to have two positions that are pretty well-developed, and three more in the pipeline. This way, as job opportunities come and go—and they always do—you've still got some hot and warm prospects. If you're trying to bubble them up at the same time, tell the others that you're "close" to a verbal offer and you were wondering what their timing might be. That will signal to them that you are interested and to get moving if they have interest in you. Try not to give them an ultimatum or say that you have an offer as they may step back and say, "Okay, go for it. We will take a pass."

This kind of approach comes naturally to sales people—they know that they need to be working ten possibilities at the same time, because, chances are, only one will hit pay dirt. Same for you. Continue to network and keep those irons in the fire. It builds capacity around your search in general. Plan a trip out of town to meet with former colleagues, clients, or customers. If you're in New York, you can easily hit Philadelphia, Stamford, Washington, D.C., or Boston. If you're in Chicago, don't overlook Minneapolis. In LA? Go to San Francisco and San Jose, too. This gets your name out there more widely, helps you keep current, and helps you bring your personal brand to the market.

The more your name is out there, the better off you are. People talking about you and seeing you as a potential connector or a resource is great. For example, Dave was unemployed but when a publicly traded company was looking to hire someone, they called him. Turns out his name had been given to them twice, in two different situations. It's less about falling in love and more about speed dating—until you get the job. Then it's the real thing. (We'll talk more about the process of onboarding at your new job in Chapter 10.)

Not being in love also helps you negotiate. Get paid at least what you made last year. Actually, start your negotiating by asking for 15% more than you made in your last job. If you don't get it, there's a good chance that you'll get at least a 10% bump. Getting a higher salary has to happen *with* a new job, not *in* a new job. It's the only time you have leverage. Be prepared to walk away (the job-hunting equivalent of the game of chicken) if they don't want to compensate you fairly. Do you really want to work at a place that undervalues its employees?

After you've landed that new job, be sure to go back and reconnect with the people you met with and who made connections for you. Now that you have a role, you have good news to share with them in person. People don't want to feel you just contacted them because you were out of work and needed something. Try to stay in touch with people when you already have a job and don't need anything. It merely takes a LinkedIn message, email, phone call or holiday card. That's true friendship.

Finally, nothing lasts forever. Same goes for this job. So stay optimistic, but keep your options open. And never, ever get complacent or stop networking. Remember the old adage, "You're not in a job, you're just between job searches."

Chapter 9

Working with Recruiters and Headhunters

At a recent networking event, Ben told the other 30 out-of-work people in the room that if he had it to do over again, he would have spent less time with recruiters. A lot less. Why? Simply put, recruiters are *not* your friends. They may woo you and may take you out to lunch, and may sound encouraging and upbeat. But they work for the employer—not for you—and they don't always have your best interests at heart. I'm not saying they're deliberately trying to deceive you—it's just that their loyalties lie with the company that will be paying their fee (which they often earn only *after* they make the placement), not with you. And in order to earn that fee, the recruiter or headhunter will wine and dine as many possible candidates as it takes. For them it's a numbers game. If they contact enough people, eventually they'll find the right candidate. With retained searches, even if an internal candidate is selected, the headhunter is paid a fee.

Unless you're very senior, or you have a very narrow focus or functionality, you should be spending 90 percent of your job-hunting time developing leads from your own network, and only 10 percent working with headhunters and recruiters.

If you do get a call from a headhunter, the first thing you want to ask is whether he or she is working on a "retained search." That means that the recruiter has an exclusive arrangement with the hiring company. In non-retained searches, the hiring company client has put the word out to a number of recruiters, and whoever brings in the right candidate gets the fee. In situations like these, the recruiter who's calling you is conducting a bit of a fishing expedition. So ask who the client (hiring company) is, what the position is, what it pays, and whether the search is retained or contingency. If they can't (or won't) answer all of those questions, don't bother sending your resume. On the other hand, if you get a sense that the recruiter is truly plugged in and has some real market intel, try to schedule a face-to-face meeting.

Once you find out the name of the company, you might discover that you're already speaking with them, or that you had submitted your resume for a job online. Coming at a company from several different directions makes you look disorganized and desperate. No employer wants to pay recruiter fees. If you made it onto their radar on your own or through your network, they'll save a lot of money (up to one third of the job's projected annual salary).

More often than not, the job a recruiter is calling about won't be right for you anyway. It might be for a position that's too junior, requires more travel than you're willing to accept, or skills you don't have. If that's the case, don't just hang up the phone. Instead, try to take advantage of having the recruiter on the phone and turn the call to your advantage.

One excellent way to do that is to recommend someone who might be a better candidate than you. If you don't know anyone, search your network and try to find someone who would be appropriate for the role. Or email or call a friend or colleague who might have an idea. That way, you'll come across as responsive, well-connected, and willing to help the recruiter land that big fee. You can be sure that the next time a position that's got your name on it comes along, that recruiter will call you first. At the same time, the person you recommended for the job may return the favor by recommending *you* for something else or giving you a great contact.

Another reason to keep the recruiter on the phone is that recruiters are great sources of market intelligence. Many of them come out of industry themselves, and they can give you the inside scoop on what's going on, whether it's something about the sector as a whole, or individual companies within that sector.

The more you talk to recruiters (and the more you listen to their market insights), the more current you'll sound when you're in meetings or interviews.

One last tip: Always be transparent in your search. If you're already talking to that firm, tell the recruiter. If they tell you about a job, *don't* go around them and approach the company directly. If you honestly hadn't met with that company before the headhunter mentioned it, let the headhunter take you in. Then you can call everyone you know there. Let the headhunter know about all of the people you know who work there now and any who used to work there. Going around a headhunter *will* backfire. You'll get a reputation in the market as someone without integrity—and that will tarnish your name, your reputation, and your brand. Do you really want to burn bridges in a tight job market or, frankly, in *any* job market?

Chapter 10

Onboard or Overboard: Settling into Your New Job

Congratulations, you're hired!

With the marketplace overflowing with highly qualified candidates who would love to have the job you just
started, it's imperative that you fit in with the culture of the
company, the team that's interviewing you, and the team
you'll actually be working with. When Barbara began her
new job at a not-for-profit, she brought the workplace habits and style that had made her a success on Wall Street.

But what had worked so well in for-profit finance was a complete flop in a very different world. Three months later Barbara was out looking for another job.

Rule Number 1:

To fit in with new people, a new job, and a new culture, "When in Rome ..."

This means that if everyone wears slacks and a button-down shirt, you should too. If everyone wears a tie, wear one. If no one does, leave yours at home. (Generally speaking, it's a good idea to dress the same way your boss does.) Since this is your first time in Rome, it's understandable that you might need a little time to get the lay of the land, and to familiarize yourself with what, exactly, those Romans are doing. So if you show up on your first day at 8:30 a.m. and everyone else is already there, you'll want to get in at 8 or 8:15 the next morning. And if it looks like most people are staying after the time you thought the workday was ending, let your spouse or your babysitter know that you'll be a few minutes late. Over the course of a few weeks, you'll be able to align your schedule with the rest of your team, department, and firm.

Rule Number 2:

Never eat alone.

Always ask someone to join you, even if you're just going down to the cafeteria to get a salad and bring it back to your desk. If everyone takes lunch at noon, you go with them. If they wait 'til 1, so do you. And don't wait to be asked out. If you see a bunch of folks about ready to head out, ask if you can join them. Try this with a few different groups of people.

Rule Number 3:

Build your network.

At least twice a day—once in the morning and once in the afternoon—get out of your chair and do some walking around. You could be heading to the restroom, coffee room, or just checking out the floor. The purpose is to say hello to at least four people during that time and remember their names. Put names with faces, faces with departments, ask basic questions like what they've got planned for the weekend, and be sure to use people's names at least once every time you speak with them. Too many times seems a bit contrived. While you're doing your walkabouts, be sure to spend some time getting to know people in other departments. Bottom line: She who knows the most people and has the biggest network, wins—or at least keeps her job longer. When there are lay-offs and senior management has to pick between two people in similar roles, the one who has the most advocates in the room, the one more people know, is more likely to be spared. Knowledge, intelligence, and producing quality work aren't always enough.

Rule Number 4:

Be a real part of the team.

You may be new on the job, but that doesn't mean you can't mentor a younger or more junior member of your team.

Puppies grow up to be dogs. Pete told me that the people who were most helpful to him in his job search were guys he had hired or mentored years before. If there's a holiday party, attend and don't get drunk. If someone's collecting for a co-worker's birthday or new baby, contribute. If someone else's daughter is selling Girl Scout cookies or candy bars for charity, buy one.

Sign every birthday card that makes the rounds and don't forget to show up in the conference room for cake. The people you work with and for must come to see you as part of the fabric of the organization. If they're looking for volunteers to help organize the company picnic, raise your hand. Believe me, they're just as curious to find out everything they can about you as you are about them. Take the mystery out of it by showing up at typical work activities. If a few colleagues are going out for a drink, join them. Even if they're from a different department or floor. You can always leave after one beer or glass of wine, saying you have to head home. Remember, never get drunk or sloppy. This is why this is called work.

Rule Number 5:

Be yourself.

Whatever you do, be absolutely sure to stay true to who you really are. That's the guy (or gal) they hired—the one they like. So just keep on being the genuine you and you'll go far.

Under the guise of this recession, companies continue to release employees who don't fit in (of course, they're also getting rid of poor performers--but that's not you.) But as I mentioned above, all things being equal, they'll retain the employee more people know and feel comfortable with.

Notes

Frequently Asked Questions

1. **How long will it take me to get a job?**
   Count on 6–12 months working on it full time—longer if you do it haphazardly.

2. **Will I make what I made last year?**
   Yes. Just ask. The market has improved a bit.

3. **Should I settle for less money/less title?**
   Generally speaking, no—unless you're switching industries or going into the not-for-profit sector instead of corporate. The one exception: is if you are in dire need. If I were in that unfortunate situation, I would wait tables if I had to. Check your budget and bank account.

4. **Should I go back more than 15 years in my resume?**
   Allocate most of the space to your accomplishments within the last 15 years. Put the rest in an Additional Work Experience section with less detailed information—but only if the firms you worked for are household names or the functions and accomplishments you did were especially wonderful and truly add something to your resume. Leave out the dates and just put in the company, your title and responsibilities, and if appropriate, one accomplishment for at least the first one—especially if it's a household name.

5. **What if I want to change industries?**
   Think honestly about skills you've developed that you think would transfer well from your old industry to a new one.

Then meet with people who work in that industry and ask them whether your proposed move makes sense to them.

6. **What do I do if I haven't been able to reach my target after three good tries (three emails, two emails and a phone call, and so on?)**

    Call someone who has a relationship (personal and/or professional) with the person you're trying to reach, and ask what's going on with your target. Then call again. Chances are it's nothing personal, and it has nothing to do with you at all. If you still get nothing but silence, send an email saying, "So sorry we weren't able to connect this year. Be well."

7. **How do I handle a panel interview?**

    Maintain eye contact with the person asking the question but keep open body language for all—no arms crossed, smile, use all of their names. This means sit up straight, face toward them, no slumping, no crossed arms.

8. **How do I handle back-to-back (sequential) interviews?**

    Be well-rested and prepared. Smile. Use everyone's name and be sure to make excellent eye contact with the person asking each question. Remember to breathe deeply, stand up and stretch in between.

9. **What do I say in the thank-you note?**

    Thank them for their time, acknowledge something they talked about in the meeting, personalize the note and ask about next steps. Always be deferential.

10. **Should I send thank-you notes to everyone I met with in a panel interview? If so, how do I make those notes different–just in case they share them with each other?**

    Yes, everyone gets a thank-you note. An email is fine, but a handwritten thank-you to the centers of influence/hiring managers might make sense and be a tipping point and differentiator for you. Make sure the first sentence is the thank-you, the second sentence is about something *they* talked about, and end with an actionable item—some kind of deliverable. For example, "Per our conversation, I will circle back to you by email late next week. I look forward to continuing our dialogue. Thanks again and best regards, Charlotte."

11. What if I don't have a "dead mouse" to bring them?

Take the meeting anyway, but know if you're not giving, you may not get much in return. What goes around, comes around. Try to give first, to get. Our society is built on the reciprocity principle. During the meeting, scope out ideas for dead mice in the future.

12. Should I have a chronological or functional resume?

Chronological.

13. How many references should I have?

Three to six, but don't include them on your resume. Be sure you've contacted them in advances and that you've given them talking points about you.

14. Who pays when I have a networking meeting?

If you invited them, you pay. If they invited you, they pay. If anyone offers, let them. You're out of work and they know that. When they are out, it will be your turn. You could also just leave the tip anytime or reach for your wallet and say "Shall we split this?"

15. How many networking meetings should I have each week?

Five to seven, face-to-face.

16. What are the most important things to focus on in an interview?

What you're good at, how it will bring value to the organization you're interviewing with. Above all, always stay positive, ask strategic, good questions, use the interviewer's name, and smile. Remember that they should be doing most of the talking, not you.

17. **What are the most important things to focus on in a networking meeting?**

    Be sure to bring your action plan with your complete list of target companies (you'll probably have 30–40 on your list). Then ask the person you're networking with whether he or she knows anyone at any of those companies, or whether he or she might be able to connect you with someone who does. Always be authentic. Build true rapport and ask what you can do for them.

18. **What else should I be doing?**

    Keep (or stay) current by reading books and magazines that are relevant to your field, attending conferences, and meeting with people who are knowledgeable about the latest industry trends. Stay fit by going to the gym, walking, biking, swimming, or whatever makes you feel good and look great—employers like that. Get involved in volunteering and community work, so you look like you're compassionate and involved in the world around you.

For one free, personalized answer to your most
burning job-hunting question,
please visit Charlotte at
www.bringadeadmouse.com.

Author Biography

Charlotte A. Lee is a Senior Vice President with Lee Hecht Harrison (LHH), the largest outplacement firm in the world with over 350 offices in 85 countries. She coaches senior executives from all industries but focuses on financial services, legal, pharma and consumer.

Prior to her role at LHH, Ms. Lee led the New York office of DBM, the first outplacement firm which had more than 400,000 clients each year. Before her work with DBM, Ms. Lee was an investment banker with Kidder, Peabody & Co, Alex Brown & Sons, and Credit Lyonnais, where she worked on debt and equity private placements, leveraged buyouts, and cross-border M&As. After investment banking, Ms. Lee formed her own firm to provide strategic planning, organizational development, sales and marketing, and career coaching to senior executives and nonprofits. She has served as the Executive Director for five nonprofits and recently led Habitat for Humanity in Nassau County as its President. She also serves on the Board of Directors of TruFund Financial and is active with the National Kidney Foundation, after donating her kidney to her sister in 2009.

Charlotte was a panelist for Fordham Law School, discussing social media and one's career, and is a frequent speaker. She has presented to GE, Deloitte, ING, State Street, PwC, Book Guilds, ASCEND, FW, Fordham Law School, Baruch College, FWA, among others. Charlotte is also active with the American Association of University

Women and founded the Munsey Park Women's Investment Club. Ms. Lee is a certified literacy tutor and has taught conversational English to Chinese-Americans for many years. Ms. Lee has appeared on CNBC, Bloomberg Radio, and NPR, and has been interviewed by the *Wall Street Journal* and *The New York Times*. She holds a Bachelor of Arts from New York University and lives in Manhasset, New York with her family.